B

by Iain Gray

Lang**Syne**

PUBLISHING

WRITING *to* REMEMBER

79 Main Street, Newtongrange,
Midlothian EH22 4NA
Tel: 0131 344 0414   Fax: 0845 075 6085
E-mail: info@lang-syne.co.uk
www.langsyneshop.co.uk

Design by Dorothy Meikle
Printed by Printwell Ltd
© Lang Syne Publishers Ltd 2016

ISBN 978-1-85217-206-0

Burns

Echoes of a far distant past
can still be found in most names

Chapter one:

Origins of
Scottish surnames

by George Forbes

It all began with the Normans.

For it was they who introduced surnames into common usage more than a thousand years ago, initially based on the title of their estates, local villages and chateaux in France to distinguish and identify these landholdings, usually acquired at the point of a bloodstained sword.

Such grand descriptions also helped enhance the prestige of these arrogant warlords and generally glorify their lofty positions high above the humble serfs slaving away below in the pecking order who only had single names, often with Biblical connotations as in Pierre and Jacques.

The only descriptive distinctions among this peasantry concerned their occupations, like Pierre the swineherd or Jacques the ferryman.

The Normans themselves were originally Vikings (or Northmen) who raided, colonised and eventually settled down around the French coastline.

They had sailed up the Seine in their long-boats in 900AD under their ferocious leader Rollo and ruled the roost in north east France before sailing over to conquer England, bringing their relatively new tradition of having surnames with them.

It took another hundred years for the Normans to percolate northwards and surnames did not begin to appear in Scotland until the thirteenth century.

These adventurous knights brought an aura of chivalry with them and it was said no damsel of any distinction would marry a man unless he had at least two names.

The family names included that of Scotland's great hero Robert De Brus and his compatriots were warriors from families like the De Morevils, De Umphravils, De Berkelais, De Quincis, De Viponts and De Vaux.

As the knights settled the boundaries of

their vast estates, they took territorial names, as in Hamilton, Moray, Crawford, Cunningham, Dunbar, Ross, Wemyss, Dundas, Galloway, Renfrew, Greenhill, Hazelwood, Sandylands and Church-hill.

Other names, though not with any obvious geographical or topographical features, nevertheless derived from ancient parishes like Douglas, Forbes, Dalyell and Guthrie.

Other surnames were coined in connection with occupations, castles or legendary deeds. Stuart originated in the word steward, a prestigious post which was an integral part of any large medieval household. The same applied to Cooks, Chamberlains, Constables and Porters.

Borders towns and forts – needed in areas like the Debateable Lands which were constantly fought over by feuding local families – had their own distinctive names; and it was often from them that the resident groups took their communal titles, as in the Grahams of Annandale, the Elliots and Armstrongs of the East Marches, the Scotts and Kerrs of Teviotdale and Eskdale.

Even physical attributes crept into surnames, as in Small, Little and More (the latter being 'beg' in Gaelic), Long or Lang, Stark, Stout, Strong or Strang and even Jolly.

Mieklejohns would have had the strength of several men, while Littlejohn was named after the legendary sidekick of Robin Hood.

Colours got into the act with Black, White, Grey, Brown and Green (Red developed into Reid, Ruddy or Ruddiman). Blue was rare and nobody ever wanted to be associated with yellow.

Pompous worthies took the name Wiseman, Goodman and Goodall.

Words intimating the sons of leading figures were soon affiliated into the language as in Johnson, Adamson, Richardson and Thomson, while the Norman equivalent of Fitz (from the French-Latin 'filius' meaning 'son') cropped up in Fitzmaurice and Fitzgerald.

The prefix 'Mac' was 'son of' in Gaelic and clans often originated with occupations – as in MacNab being sons of the Abbot, MacPherson and MacVicar being sons of the minister and MacIntosh being sons of the chief.

The church's influence could be found in the names Kirk, Clerk, Clarke, Bishop, Friar and Monk. Proctor came from a church official, Singer and Sangster from choristers, Gilchrist and Gillies from Christ's servant, Mitchell, Gilmory and Gilmour from servants of St Michael and Mary, Malcolm from a servant of Columba and Gillespie from a bishop's servant.

The rudimentary medical profession was represented by Barber (a trade which also once included dentistry and surgery) as well as Leech or Leitch.

Businessmen produced Merchants, Mercers, Monypennies, Chapmans, Sellers and Scales, while down at the old village watermill the names that cropped up included Miller, Walker and Fuller.

Other self explanatory trades included Coopers, Brands, Barkers, Tanners, Skinners, Brewsters and Brewers, Tailors, Saddlers, Wrights, Cartwrights, Smiths, Harpers, Joiners, Sawyers, Masons and Plumbers.

Even the scenery was utilised as in Craig, Moor, Hill, Glen, Wood and Forrest.

Rank, whether high or low, took its place with Laird, Barron, Knight, Tennant, Farmer, Husband, Granger, Grieve, Shepherd, Shearer and Fletcher.

The hunt and the chase supplied Hunter, Falconer, Fowler, Fox, Forrester, Archer and Spearman.

The renowned medieval historian Froissart, who eulogised about the romantic deeds of chivalry (and who condemned Scotland as being a poverty stricken wasteland), once sniffily dismissed the peasantry of his native France as the jacquerie (or the jacques-without-names) but it was these same humble folk who ended up over-throwing the arrogant aristocracy.

In the olden days, only the blueblooded knights of antiquity were entitled to full, proper names, both Christian and surnames, but with the passing of time and a more egalitarian, less feudal atmosphere, more respectful and worthy titles spread throughout the populace as a whole.

Echoes of a far distant past can still be found in most names and they can be borne with pride in commemoration of past generations who fought and toiled in some capacity or other to make our nation what it now is, for good or ill.

Chapter two:

Kindred of the clan

The surname of Burns has understandably become synonymous with that of Scotland's great national bard, Robert Burns: but generations of others of the name have also made an indelible mark not only on the pages of Scotland's dramatic story but on the international stage.

Ironically for a name that has such a strong resonance for Scots, its roots lie in the Old English word 'burn', or 'bourne', meaning 'stream', and indicating someone who lived near a stream, or burn.

A rather more martial derivation, however, is that it stems from the Old English 'beorn', meaning 'warrior.'

Varieties of spelling have included Burn, Burness, Bernis, and Bernes, and the form 'Burns' does not appear in Scottish records until the seventeenth century.

The singular form of 'Burn', however, was popular in Dumfriesshire and the Borders as early as the thirteenth and fourteenth centuries.

This singular form gradually gave way from the early nineteenth century onwards to the more common form of 'Burns', owing to the widespread popularity of the poet.

The form 'Burness' was to be found in Kincardineshire, in the east of Scotland, where the poet's father, William, was born and raised.

He later moved to Ayrshire, where his famous son was born in 1759, and it was in 1786 that Robert and his brother Gilbert changed their name from Burness to Burns.

Both Burns and Burness are recognised by some sources as septs, or having kinship with, the proud Clan Campbell, and the reasons for this still remain something of a rather controversial historical mystery, with several conflicting explanations.

One of these is that a family of Burnses (the plural form of Burns) were already settled in

Ayrshire sometime before the poet's family settled there, and that they owed allegiance to the Campbell earls of Loudoun.

A rather more complex, but suitably romantic explanation, however, takes us back to Taynuilt, at the head of Loch Awe, in Argyll, the ancestral homeland of the Campbells: it is also an explanation to which immediate descendants of the poet appear to have subscribed, at least for a time.

It was at Taynuilt, at some undetermined date in the early to mid seventeenth century, or perhaps even much earlier, that a family of Campbells were one day visited by a band of bards, or rhymers.

Highland communities held bards in high esteem because they were the valued and cherished custodians of a clan's proud heritage and tradition.

By ancient custom, these wandering bands of poets could claim free board and lodging wherever they decided to visit, quite literally for the price of a song.

On the day they visited the Campbell home at Taynuilt a son of the house, Walter, was busily engaged in the hard task of splitting a log of wood by driving a wedge along its length when a band of bards arrived.

Promising them refreshment after he had finished his labours, he asked them to put their hands into the gap already opened up in the log, to help to pull it further apart.

The poets, although not accustomed to manual labour, readily obliged, but Walter, annoyed at the prospect of his family having to entertain them, struck the wedge a mighty blow with his hammer, driving it right through the log.

This resulted in the edges springing tightly together, leaving the fingers of the bards' painfully trapped.

As they howled in pain, Walter said he would free them only if they agreed to leave his home and seek refreshment elsewhere.

They readily agreed, but later raised such a hue and cry over the inhospitable treatment they had received that Walter was forced to flee the area and seek a new life elsewhere.

The treatment meted out to the bards could have been much worse: an Act was passed in 1616 in a desperate attempt to curb the lawlessness then prevalent in the Highlands and Islands, and among its many provisions was that bards should be treated in the same way as beggars and other 'idlers.'

They were to be imprisoned, their ears cut off and banished, facing death by hanging if they returned!

Walter Campbell, meanwhile, is said to have fled east across the country to Kincardineshire and, for added safety, changed his name to 'Burnhouse'.

This, in turn, was later changed to the already existing local name of 'Burness.'

The reason he chose the name Burnhouse, it is argued, is that 'Taynuilt', his original home, stems from the Gaelic 'Tigh-an-Uillt', meaning 'house of the burn', or 'burnhouse', and meant he could retain a link with his past.

Some sources maintain that this tale (a rather ironical one bearing in mind the fame of Robert Burns as a poet) is entirely spurious, but it is one that Burns's family appear to have believed – to the extent that in 1837 a descendant of the poet who was employed with the Honourable East India Company was granted arms by the Lord Lyon King of Arms of Scotland that included one of the Clan Campbell armorial devices.

Less than fifteen years later, however, he dropped this device from his arms, and some sources argue this was because new evidence had come to light that disproved the Campbell link.

The truth of the matter may never be known, but the tradition of a Burness/Burns kinship with the clan is so strong that many feel they are entitled to share in the clan's heritage.

Such a link would mean that generations of Burnses shared in not only Clan Campbell's glorious fortunes, but also its tragic misfortunes.

Chapter three:

Freedom fighters and reivers

A wild boar is the crest of Clan Campbell, an ancient clan that claims a descent from Diarmid, slayer of a venomous boar and one of whose descendants, Gillespie Campbell, was granted the lordship of Loch Awe, in Argyll, towards the end of the thirteenth century.

Four main branches of the powerful clan emerged, all with their own proud motto: the Campbells of Argyll have the motto 'Forget not'; 'Follow me' is the motto of the Campbells of Breadalbane, 'Be mindful' that of the Campbells of Cawdor, while 'I bide my time' is the motto of the Campbells of Loudoun.

The main seat of the Campbells of Argyll was for centuries at Loch Awe, but their base moved towards the end of the fifteenth century to Inveraray, near Loch Fyne.

In 1457 Colin, the 2nd Lord Campbell, was created the 1st Earl of Argyll.

The Campbells were resolute in their support of the cause of Scotland's freedom during the bitter and bloody Wars of Independence with England, and it was Sir Neil Campbell of Lochawe, who married Robert the Bruce's sister, Mary, who fought at the side of the great warrior king along with his clansmen and kinsmen at the battle of Bannockburn in 1314.

By midsummer of 1313 the mighty fortress of Stirling Castle was occupied by an English garrison under the command of Sir Philip Mowbray, and Bruce's brother, Edward, rashly agreed to a pledge by Mowbray that if the castle was not relieved by battle by midsummer of the following year, then he would surrender.

This made battle inevitable, and by June 23 of 1314 the two armies faced one another at Bannockburn, in sight of the castle.

It was on this day that Bruce slew the English knight Sir Henry de Bohun in single combat, but the battle proper was not fought until the following day, shortly after the mid-summer sun had risen.

The English cavalry launched a desperate but futile charge on the densely packed ranks of Scottish spearmen known as schiltrons, and by the time the sun had sank slowly in the west the English army had been totally routed, with Edward himself only narrowly managing to make his escape from the carnage of the battlefield.

An equally terrible defeat was inflicted on the Scots in 1513, however, when up to 5000 Scots, including James IV, an archbishop, two bishops, eleven earls, fifteen barons, and 300 knights were slain at the battle of Flodden after the monarch had crossed the border into England.

Included in the ranks of the Scots were about 7,500 clansmen, including Archibald Campbell, the 2nd Earl of Argyll, who fell along with his clansmen and kinsmen.

It was under the command of another Earl of Argyll that fifty-five years later, in May of 1568, an army loyal to the ill-starred Mary, Queen of Scots, was defeated at the battle of Langside, on the southern outskirts of Glasgow.

Archibald Campbell, the 8th Earl of Argyll, and who was created 1st Marquis of Argyll in 1641, was the Covenanting leader who fought against the Royalist forces led by John Graham, 1st Marquis of Montrose, during his great campaigns from 1644 to 1645, in support of Charles I and in opposition to the Covenanting authorities.

The Covenanters had taken their name from the National Covenant, first signed in the Greyfriars kirkyard in Edinburgh in February of 1638 in defence of the Presbyterian religion and in opposition to the king's claim of supremacy in matters of religion.

The earl was forced to ignominiously flee to safety in his galley after Montrose wiped out 1,500 of his Covenanters in a daring surprise attack on Inverlochy on February 2, 1645.

What made the victory all the more remarkable was that Montrose and his hardy band had arrived at Inverlochy after a gruelling 36-hour march south through knee-deep snow from the area of present-day Fort Augustus.

Success followed again for the earl's bitter enemy at Kilsyth on August 15, 1645, but Montrose was finally defeated at Philiphaugh, near Selkirk, less than a month later.

While those of the name of Burns shared in both the many successes and failures of the mighty Clan Campbell, their namesakes in the Borders (who used the singular form of 'Burn'), had for centuries been gaining a rather notorious reputation for themselves as one of the many riding clans, or reivers.

These reivers took their name from their lawless custom of reiving, or raiding, not only their neighbours' livestock, but also that of their neighbours across the border.

The word 'bereaved', for example, indicating to have suffered loss, derives from the original 'reived', meaning to have suffered loss of property.

The Treaty of York had been signed by Scotland's Alexander II in 1237, establishing the border with England as a line running from the

Solway to the Tweed, but until as late as the seventeenth century the Borders became a byword for lawlessness.

There were three Marches, or areas of administration, on either side of the border – the West, Middle, and East Marches – all governed by a warden.

On the Scottish side of the border, the East March was dominated by the Homes and Swintons, with the Kerrs, Douglases, and Elliots holding sway in the Middle March, and the Armstrongs, Maxwells and Johnstones in control of the West March.

The host of minor families, such as the family of Burn, allied themselves to particular stronger families, and, in the case of the Burns, this was with the Elliot clan of the Middle March.

Complaints from either side of the border, and there were many, were dealt with on Truce Days, with the wardens of the respective marches acting as arbitrators, while under a special law known as the Hot Trod, anyone who had their livestock stolen had the right to pursue the thieves and regain their property at the point of the sword.

In many cases, however, the wardens of the marches were far from arbitrary in their rulings, with self-interest governing their decisions, and as a result the Borders remained a scene of virtual anarchy, with no respect for royal authority.

The Burns, for example, are said to have summarily slain seventeen members of the rival Collingwood family after a Collingwood killed one of their own number.

The infamous and hot-blooded Geordie Burn, meanwhile, who was hanged for his nefarious activities in 1596, confessed before his execution that he had spent a life of 'whoring, drinking, stealing and taking deep revenge for slight offences'!

This state of lawlessness remained almost endemic until James VI, following the Union of the Crowns in 1603, asserted his authority and, in later centuries, generations of Burnses pursued rather more peaceful pursuits, achieving lasting acclaim in a number of fields.

Chapter four:

Poetic legacy

Undoubtedly the most famous of those to have borne the proud surname of Burns is the poet whose birth on January 25, 1759, in a humble cottage in Alloway, Ayrshire, is celebrated annually at countless Burns Suppers across the world.

It should come as no surprise that more than two hundred years after his tragically young death, at the age of 37, that Burns should still retain such an international appeal, because his voice is that of the common man and woman and articulates basic human sentiments shared by all.

From *The Cottar's Saturday Night* and *Green Grow the Rashes* to *Tam O'Shanter* and *The Tree of Liberty*, his poems and songs cover an entire array of human emotions, and these feelings of love, joy, heartbreak, and despair were ones that the poet himself experienced deeply at various stages throughout his short life.

He was still a humble farmer when the now priceless Kilmarnock Edition of his works, *Poems, Chiefly in the Scottish Dialect*, was published on July 31, 1786, and by the end of the following month only 13 of the original 612 copies printed still remained.

He had netted a profit of about £20 and planned to use this towards his travel expenses to take up a post as a bookkeeper at Port Antonio in Jamaica.

The poet was heartbroken at the prospect of having to depart Scottish shores, but it seemed he had very few other options left: his farm at Mossgiel was a financial albatross around his neck, despite all his backbreaking work, while his sweetheart, Jean Armour of Mauchline, was pregnant with the twins she would give birth to in September.

With Burns in dire financial straits and harried by Jean's disapproving family, it was his plan to depart for Jamaica in a desperate bid to earn enough to support a family.

His vessel had been lying at Greenock for several weeks, but its departure, fortunately for posterity, kept being postponed.

On September 4, 1786, as Burns nervously waited for a sailing date, he received news that influential members of Edinburgh's literary society had ecstatically received the edition, and this proved crucial in his decision to abandon his plans to emigrate and gave him the necessary encouragement to pursue a career as a poet.

Accordingly, he unpacked his bags for the West Indies and, on November 27, 1786, riding a borrowed pony, set off from Ayrshire to Edinburgh where, by April of the following year, another edition of his work was published, proving to be the late eighteenth century equivalent of a bestseller, with 3,000 copies printed and 2,800 of these being bought by 1,500 subscribers.

Perilous financial circumstances meant that Burns needed a more steady income, however, and through the help of patrons he obtained the lease of a farm at Ellisland, near the town of Dumfries, and employment as a gauger, or exciseman.

His work required him to ride up to thirty or forty miles a day, and this placed an added strain on his already fragile health. Still writing to the last, he died in Dumfries on July 21, 1796, and was buried in the town's St. Michael's Cemetery.

Burns was a staunch advocate and defender of human rights and another Burns, born in Brooklyn, New York, in 1879, devoted her life to the American movement for women's rights. This was Lucy Burns, who was also a vociferous opponent of the First World War.

In the world of commerce, Sir George Burns, born in Glasgow in 1795, was the entrepreneur who, along with his brother James, formed the basis of the shipping company that today operates across the west coast of Scotland as Caledonian MacBrayne.

The brothers were also involved in what led to the creation of the mighty Cunard Line of passenger vessels.

In the world of sport Tommy Burns, born in Glasgow in 1956, is the former professional footballer and manager who was signed to Celtic Football Club in 1973.

Although the surname of Burnside has its own heritage and traditions, bearers of the name can be loosely regarded as kin of the great community of Burnses.

A Clan Burnside was recorded in Angus in the sixteenth century and in Stirlingshire in the seventeenth century.

Born in London in 1852, William Burnside was a celebrated English mathematician, while Ambrose Everett Burnside, born in 1824 in Liberty, Indiana, founded the company that produced the famous Burnside breech-loading rifle.

As a Union general in the American Civil War, however, he was best known for a luxuriant growth of facial hair that joined his ears to his moustache but left the chin clean-shaven. These became known as 'burnsides', more commonly known today as 'sideburns'!

A Man's A Man For A' That

by Robert Burns

Is there for honest Poverty
That hings his head, an' a' that;
The coward slave-we pass him by,
We dare be poor for a' that!
For a' that, an' a' that.
Our toils obscure an' a' that,
The rank is but the guinea's stamp,
The Man's the gowd for a' that.

What though on hamely fare we dine,
Wear hoddin grey, an' a that;
Gie fools their silks, and knaves their wine;
A Man's a Man for a' that:
For a' that, and a' that,
Their tinsel show, an' a' that;
The honest man, tho' e'er sae poor,
Is king o' men for a' that.

Ye see yon birkie, ca'd a lord,
Wha struts, an' stares, an' a' that;

Tho' hundreds worship at his word,
He's but a coof for a' that:
For a' that, an' a' that,
His ribband, star, an' a' that:
The man o' independent mind
He looks an' laughs at a' that.

A prince can mak a belted knight,
A marquis, duke, an' a' that;
But an honest man's abon his might,
Gude faith, he maunna fa' that!
For a' that, an' a' that,
Their dignities an' a' that;
The pith o' sense, an' pride o' worth,
Are higher rank than a' that.

Then let us pray that come it may,
(As come it will for a' that,)
That Sense and Worth, o'er a' the earth,
Shall bear the gree, an' a' that.
For a' that, an' a' that,
It's coming yet for a' that,
That Man to Man, the world o'er,
Shall brothers be for a' that.